rocky-o

grind central station

America Star Books
Frederick, Maryland

© 2016 by rocky-o.
All rights reserved. No part of this book may be reproduced, stored in a retrieval system or transmitted in any form or by any means without the prior written permission of the publishers, except by a reviewer who may quote brief passages in a review to be printed in a newspaper, magazine or journal.

First printing

America Star Books has allowed this work to remain exactly as the author intended, verbatim, without editorial input.

Hardcover 9781683941361
Softcover 9781682905418
PUBLISHED BY AMERICA STAR BOOKS, LLLP
www.americastarbooks.pub
Frederick, Maryland

...bohemian paraphrase...

art, for some, is entertainment,

others wish to think...

i am mostly of the second mind,

decidedly engrossed by the visceral way

something can make me feel inside,

rather than any external jubilation

it could apply...

i prefer art not to go down easy,

like an alcoholic beverage that one forgets
they ever had

when they get behind the wheel to drive...

i want art to drive me...

i want it to be like sandpaper that,

while course in its application, can also,

in the long term, smooth out the rough edges

of my very existence,

with its very existence...

...and so...it exists...it all exists...

influences...i have plenty...

in life, we are always experiencing,
always learning...

these things make-up our make-up...

the places we go...like bohack and the automat

the events that shape our lives...like
woodstock and watergate...

authors like agatha christie, rod serling,
and sir arthur conan doyle...

journalists like chris welch and carl bernstein...

directors like robert altman, woody allen and
terry gilliam...

songwriters like sting, bob marley,
and david gilmore...

singer/songwriter friends like jacob steele and
joey monteleone...

friends like jo morris (street)...kera jenkins
(bridge)...
and bonnie jackson (light)...

...

and, as always, my angel carol...

and, of course, the holy spirit,
whose generosity knows no bounds, because...

i am not a good writer...

i'm simply a blessed one...

...peace always...

TABLE OF CONTENTS

...prologue...

...mannahattan...
—

the sand has scraped against my soul,

wearing away the night and day...

but the trace of oasis still exists,

for i've tasted fertile soil once again,

and my soul cannot resist...

i breathed again, thru paper and pen...

all spirits in a row, from head to toe...

alive, i cry...alive, i am...

the great i am, how late i am...

time once restrained, has now been retained,

as the pendulum regains its swing to the bliss...

for i've tasted fertile soil once again...

and my soul knows not to resist...

...awaiting the melting...
—

i have died many times...and rose again...

i am not the same person i was before...

                  or before that...

                                    or before that...

though each time, i bring forward with me
something not left behind me...

...and each time a little more...

but then, surrounded by the ashes of what was,
now is...

and within that flame, what remains is what i am...

...till i die again...

...chapter one...

...one way beat...
—

the sun rose today, again, over the trees and the
hills that exist
somewhere in the world...
and thru my fire escape i can see the streets of
grey that lead the
way, finally dry, to another day...
captured by the moment when my body decides
to have a mind of its
own, i stretch to see how far i can reach...
but my reach is short compared to His, and thank
God it is...
it's what can get me out of bed, it allows me to do so...
call it faith, call it experience, call it whatever you
like, i don't need proof
by some term or definition...
it's part of a condition...i simply know...
and that's good enough...ya' know...

...another chelsea morning...
—

another chelsea morning...another cup of coffee...

...to rest my head in...again...

sippin' and sittin' in the hotel coffee shop, i had to
stop while the feeling

was hot...

part spirit, part flesh...

...but therein lies the test...

and my table stands firm on its circular path...

part donut, part album...

...no problem here...

and i heard the news today, about another place
    that's gone away...

the empire's closed, the chelsea is sold...

another chelsea morning...another cup of coffee...

...shhhwoop...
—

slow, smokey, quiver...

—

in the bass of forgiveness...

—

the lines have been drawn...

—

in two-bit quarter-time...
—

and each line, and each note...

—

vibrates to justify...

—

the meaning of a beating heart...

—

and the reasons telling why...

...echo home...
—

oh delicate siren, you're calling me home

to greet my fair maiden, who's living alone

the sea has been blessing me, all of my life

but now i must make my way, back to my wife

oh delicate siren, the rocks i approach

but upon the shoreline, i can see a ghost

a man i once knew, and hope to again

for upon the shoreline, i once called him friend

oh delicate siren, i must this bequeath

to steer cross the causeway, and down past the reef

though the sea has been blessing me all of my life

it's time that i give my soul, back to my wife

...metro dustbowl...
—

these are my streets...this is my city...

people try to take it away...

people try to destroy it...

but the neon and skyscrapers are all window dressing

to the message underneath...

there is a flavor that hangs in the air...

there is an essence in those who call themselves

born-n-bred here...

there is a hunger and a way to be fed...
there is a lamppost, straight up ahead...

these are my streets...this is my city...

...bound for glory...

—

mark and twain stood by the drain,
waiting for the earth to stand still...

the melting of the snow,
is slow at the going,
but not at all by the lax...

george and orwell, across the street
stood and stared at the two
as they prayed for heat

but the melting of the snow,
in question as this
for the fortress abundant,
was simply a kiss...

...cityscrape...

—

the heat of the city street contradicts the cool of the brick, as it lies in wait for the next soul to come upon it...

tired, achy, restless...the muse of new york has taken a break from all its worth and struggle...

but who's to know what's left of the shuffle, when life begins anew...

and what to do...what to do...

terrorized, liquidized, humilitized, homogenized...

all for the paper to be clean once again...for the dirt to be swept away...for a spotless world to live in, removing the ink from the previous page, so that the words won't get in the way...

but who's to blame...

the woman looking out her window watching the world go by...the t-shirt with the coffee stain that can't be removed, yet still freshly laundered and flapping in the breeze...

the siren in the distance, that seems to be always
     coming closer…or the corner newsstand, where
     your morning paper always has a corner bent,
     a tear, a rip…

the world is dirty…and it is ripped…and it is filled
     with words that need to be heard regardless…in
     spite of…or because of…

...all that's jazzed...
—

"sure. i'd love some", i said,
noticing that our waitress had the most
beautiful pair of eyes i'd ever seen.

and they were the kind
you really couldn't help but notice, no matter
who you were...

she was also wearing
a really cool sweatshirt that had the club's logo on
   it...

and so...
before the night was done...

i bought one...

...blues as necessary...

—

the quiet of mind, searches my soul,
                to engage in any rhyme or banter
            that it may come across...
                        but there is loss...

a tender loss right now,
            that sees a whole that's grown so fowl...

not a complacency,
                    per se...
        more like ambiguity that has gotten in the way...

but it's o.k...
                for i know i know i know
                            that everything's o.k...

        ...blues as necessary...blessings always...

...smoke...
—

smoke gets in your eyes...and you wonder why...

sad eyed lady of the lower east side, contemplating
    the world around you

that has found you weeping, and crying...wondering
    how you are going to

feed your baby tonite...

but it's alright...

they say a change is gonna come, but for many or
    just for one...no one

seems sure, except the present seems sure that it
    isn't going to be you...

but you'll make it thru...you always do...

somehow, someway…

and maybe tomorrow will be better…

…you've already given up on today…

...stations...
—

looking thru a window
that's a splinter of my time
the blur of every platform brings
another thought to mind

i gaze upon the consciousness
of things i've yet to find
cause here i'm still an immigrant
to something so divine

calling out the locals
looking at the floor
i cannot seem to separate
the soundtrack from the score

i try to stand on reason
but reason's put to shame
when all that you hold sacred
is a point of new exchange

cause the rails seem to know the way to go
even if i have to question all i know
like broken windows, that cannot, hold their frames
we rely upon, whatever, remains...

looking thru the window
at a picture of my life
the blur of every platform brings
another peace of mind...

i gaze upon the emptiness
of things i leave behind
cause here i'm still an immigrant
to something so divine...

...beneath...
—

...beneath...

beneath the bleak grey skies,

i see,

bleak grey streets...

and beneath the bleak grey streets,

i see...

bleak grey people...

how far beneath

must we go

to see the light...

...every one waiting...

—

my eyes are open...

they appear to be, when they are not...

and what is what...when i seemingly stare at something or someone, and

all the while, i'm in a world of my own...

...and i can see clearly in there...

...arch...

—

discern this certain eulogy

—

a crust of bread for us to eat

—

to correlate the idol throne

—

capitulate what's truly known

—

to bark upon the branches light

—

to trample down the vineyards right

—

to gain a grace that's yet to peak

—

discern this certain eulogy

...orange...
—

i know all the plots and plans,
the pots and pans
that i go into...

i know all the schemes and dreams,
that line and define
and draw us into a place
unknown to us...

i conceive and believe
in the deception and collection
of one's inner soul,
making it half-way whole...

i pressure and measure
the inclination of the situation,
based upon a study done
by those more competent than i...

but i...

i know the plots and the plans,
the pots and the pans
of this world that i'm under...

...trite flabbergast of the ponderous circumstance...

—

it's 3:30 in the morning and i'm trying to capture lightning in a bottle...

it's snowing outside, but that doesn't help...

so...as i sit here trying not to repeat myself, i repeat and repeat and repeat because i have nothing better to say...i think i spoiled myself last friday...

that's when the holy spirit took over, so i know the difference...

and this ain't it...

cast aside something or other...i don't know...

harken down the mizzenmast and throw down the sea of raging inconsistencies for yonder lights the veil of mass destruction according to thine own self be true...ahhh, therein lies the hoastable foastable...

and ghostable equity rages on against the machine,
against the system that beats you down with
improprieties and abnormalities and whatever
else sounds good with those two other words…

why not…what does it all mean…where is it all
going…does any of this really go anywhere…

i'll know tomorrow…

...season...
—

my fingers hurt when they bend...my eyes can
    barely open
my blood constricts just like ice...flowing thru
    cold waters

and the ever-present sting...of a pick upon the strings
blows frozen wings of doubt over me
and the slow-motion time...in which I find myself
leaves me viced, and it's hard for me to breathe

but I can see my breath...and it scares me half to death
i can see my breath...is it all that I have left

my flesh is cracking at the bone...it's unwelcome
    upon me
my lips are dry from my soul...there's an echo that
    surrounds me

and the ever-present quiver of 10,000 arrows shivering
a million silver-tips of doubt on me
and the slow-motion time, of which I can't deny
leaves me viced, and it's hard for me to breathe...

but I can see my breath...and it scares me half to death
I can see my breath...is it all that I have left

…bitter almonds…
—

this garden party of weeds and things makes me
believe the woodshed is not long for the calling…

the banal meets the inane thru words and phrases
'tween the pages…and they repeat…to no one's
amazement including my own…

for twigs and twags and gallylags of tongues that
wag upon the effervescence of condensed
clouds, only suffice to blanket the world from
the nourishment it deserves…

and what becomes…the flowers not bloom and the
sheets dare not dry…but the wind still blows
towards what end but roses upon thy cheeks
and little more…

what must be cut to the quick to deny thy branches
to fall, they stem not to rot…

forget the forgotten frills and daffodils of yesterday's
belongings and petal's warnings that sit boldly
upon your crown and keep you from falling down…

to stand at attention is a mere suggestion when it
comes to the dash of haberdashery…for what is
the worth of a hat, if there is nothing beneath…

...angel number nineteen...
—

is that the phone ringing?...did i hear an angel singing?...

was that the church bell once again?...

did i have to really suffer?...do you have an answer mother?...

was it the price to pay for hell?...

what am i missing here...what is it all about...

do i have to choose...is it just win or lose...

don't they know how much we suffer...don't they know how time is muffled on...

...and before you know it, it's gone...

but hold on...

there's a crack in the bell...there's no message on the phone...

the angel flew too close, and now she's lost and so alone...

don't they know how much we need her...couldn't
  anybody feed her...

'cause before ya' know it, she's gone...

...solace...

—

i see it in your dna...

i see your color palate, dark and grey...

a sliver of white is caught by the light of a passing streetlamp you walk beneath...

it's cold...

your shawl is nearly all you have to keep you warm...to give you shelter from the storm...

but this is the norm for you here...

it's dark...it's night...with only that slim light to guide you, though you know where you are going...

the footsteps in the snow are a good indication of your current destination...

there's little variation in your day, or in your way...

it's all the same...

…anyunderground…
—

as i made my way down the stairs, my eyes adjusted from neo-classic to neon, as i stared down the darkened tunnel to see if i could hear…

the murmured echo was simply the score to an already proven air, but as yet to engage was the add-on, to which my purpose of being there would achieve…

the turnstile engaged me momentarily, as the click-click click seemed to sustain me into thinking that this was something new, that i'd never seen before…

or perhaps the rodded door, that looks more like a torture device that an exit to paradise…but who knew…

digitized and homogenized, the token of my once affection has seen better days, merely to be replaced upon its long-standing perch, and lurch into history's refrain…

and here comes the train…

clickety-clackety, clickety-clackety…the glide of steel awaits me with a thrill, a smile in which

to engage my every senses...and pretenses, for,
i know i've been there before...but still, it is a
thrill once more...

and as i enter the open door, i am greeted by a
passenger who knows so much more...and one
who is seeking...

...someone engaged, with plans for the asking...

...and one with a word to share with the rest of the
class...

...until the next station pass...

...angie...
—

look at those eyes
starin' over the newspaper
look that says that i'll see you later
but for now, enjoy the ride

look at those hands
as they press the press with confidence
underlining the last sentence
of a story, left to time

headline read
that the government lied to us again
who knows what else
the adverts are reruns as well

look at the way
she turns the page with experience
for words, right now, i am at a loss
guess she's been here before on this line

look at the time
her watch says that her stop is here
but for me, it is very clear
that i'll be here for some time

headline read
that the number of homeless is rising again
who knows what else
the adverts are reruns as well

...jester (a-side)...
—

there's a stop sign ahead, that says to go back
and there's a preacher hitchhiking wherever he can
and the gravel by the roadside don't leave nothin'
    to chance
for the commonwealth prisoner asking to dance

the kingdom is set-up and dressed up to nines
for the expected one who arrives just in time
the woman are fainting with fans draped in hand
and the tune playing was never told to the band

but the royalty duly elected
sat proudly upon their conjecture
with arms open wide, the gates alibied
the tune that was pre-selected
the face on the crowd turned into a frown
cause they never expected the jester
no they weren't expecting the jester

the spears they were gleaming for god's chosen one
but the arrogant slacker arrived for some fun
to fill in the void of the preacher annoyed
left standing by the road
left standing all alone

while the jokerman entertained troops one by one
the king he sat quietly twiddling thumbs
and the duke was nowhere to be found
and the queen, she was not around
but he fiddled with this, and he praddled with that
on occassion he even would bow and tip hat
and the spears they were lowered for all did agree
he was more than polite company

and the royalty duly elected
raised hands to reveal all their pleasure
with arms open wide, he was welcomed inside
to the circle that was never mentioned
and the face on the crowd approved with abound
and they all protected the jester
yes, they stopped protesting the jester

...jester (b-side)...
—

...then late after dark, a window had broken
inside the queen's chambers, a man's voice had spoken
the queen she had laid and played fast asleep
but it wasn't her soul that the good lord would keep
cause the preacher never made it, to join in the gala
of the jester's arrival, in place of god's favor
and the duke, someone thought he spied
to keep the queen occupied

and the royalty duly elected
was swayed to play out as suggested
with arms open wide, and his thumb down with pride
the duke was duly corrected
and the face on the crowd, joined in to be proud
for justice had found its redemption
but truth be told, the vengeance served cold
never really answered the question
cause they never suspected the jester
no, they never suspected the jester

cause the royalty duly elected
raised hands to reveal all their pleasure
with arms open wide, all were welcomed inside
from that nite on, it was never mentioned
and the face on the crowd approved with abound
never knowing they protected the jester
no, they never suspected the jester

...dancing with the kid...
—

subway darkness skips a beat as the frames of
  reference flash by to

develop the film before our eyes...

there's no disguise, as we press against the rails
  upon the rails that train

our decisions to be more patient, and comfortable...

but comfort can be disguised by the press of the
  day, shadowing overcast

looks upon unsuspecting strangers...as music
  begins to play...

the score, for which is heard time and again,
  repeats and repeats in our

ears, leaving little else to hear beyond our own
  intentions...

but since rejections can manipulate whatever we
    anticipate, that casts

the epitaph of our consciousness to pure
    emotionless...

and what appears to be a wooden bridge, shaky
    within its construction,

amasses to be a conduit for the spirit to continue
    to move throughout...

of that there is no doubt...

...it takes a village...
—

blessings
slip forth and
back to back
as my cup
of straight black
rises in the steam
of a dream
yet...

i know
there's a street
beyond this world...

...unfinished symph...
—

the grip is all packed, the train's at the station

the temperature's rising, beyond expectation

the operator's gone, the drugstore is closed...

the bookshelf is empty, the percolator dozed...

the directions are clear, the roadmap's at hand

the treasure is waiting, not sunken in sand

the doors have been locked, and the lights are
extinguished

the path has been cleared, and the worries
relinquished

the tired ol' dime, has slipped from our slacks

the engine divine, awaits on the tracks

...chapter two...

...in the beginning...

—

where will it all end...on a road, on a bend...

will i be lying in bed, or lying to a friend...

will i be captivated by the press...or found wholly half-dressed...

where will it all end...

not that i sit and contemplate, day after day, my final day...

it's just as i get closer, i start to supposer more and more, i guess...

will i be remembered here on earth...will i be remembered up above...

is my elevator going north, or somewhere undiscovered...

do i even have to contemplate, this most rote of all the rituals...

to sit and wonder of one's fate, when time's become habitual...

the grey hair strands i wear with pride...

the aches and pains i try to hide...

the plans that seem to have no time...

this is why, i wonder why again...

where will it all end...

...bonedripper...

—

soaked to the bone...waiting for a bus...

the rain hasn't stopped since as long as i can remember...

and i can remember pretty long...

but now my mind seems to be forgetting things...
going blank as time moves forward...

what's the case just like the rain...constant...
abandoned...

each drop represents something, as if hanging
by the edge of my nose is significant to its
existence...

and what of mine...

am i like that drop...eventually joining the collective
to make my way down the unfathomable gutter
that lays waiting below, only to be streamed
into a consciousness of none...

and then...gone...

there must be more, as i stand here in the rain,
waiting for a bus...

soaked to the bone...

...loosen the noose...

—

have you ever tried to plant a donut, just to watch
it grow?...

there has to be a certain pathos in the rhythm,
surely as there must be a

little levity in the rhyme...

and holy spirit rocks all the time, and in this spot
i dwell in...

is it just me?...or a bubbling well, that, in itself,
spills from a certain

place...

a geological wonder of time and space...

god's little pinpoint for his nephew to choose...

win or lose, it's all about the game...

...greenwich avenue pause...

—

while 'neath a sky not so inviting
i heard an ancient call
and in my mind, it kept reciting
so near, so far, the fall

the corners dark, alive at night
the daily blindness of the light
the shepherds watch of sheep so tightly
coursed throughout this meadow

and as we watch the children play
with soft turned focus slipped away
for all around, there is at bay
a certain air of feeling

while 'neath that sky, so uninviting
we hear the ancient howl
of packs that cry, into the sky
yet never make a sound

the pressure up against the stone
that's carved by lives in multi-tones
layed down by those, yet found alone
on courses of this meadow

and as we watch the world turn swift
with soft raised eyes, we gently lift
our heads up to the skies adrift
in certain airs of feeling...

...rose know thorns...

—

a joy, in never stillness comes...

for lying in wait is evergreen mounted on a isle in
the willow...

and there, on thy pillow, lies a rose...

a rose that has no thorns, no aroma to speak of at
all...just plain, and simple, to look at...

it adorns the white as crimson will...it nestles itself
like a comforting lamb, laid out at the feet of the
master...

and oh the joy...

sorrow knows not of this pillow, for it has held
many a head firmly in its breath...

...and allows them to breathe again...

for but that single rose...imposing itself like the
crest of a wave against the shoreline rocks that
lay ever so mightily in traditions steep...

and now, to sleep...protected, provided, in comfort,
i lie here...

adorned...by a rose with no thorns...

...ninety-nine point nine...
—

the ink has not run out yet...

and so,

i am compelled to write again...

to instigate,

investigate,

repeat, rinse, repeat...

whatever it takes...

as long as pen holds to paper

and streams thru my being,

i am immensely grateful

to the infinite seeing me thru...

but the end of the page

is my refrain

as soon, i shall simply

turn the page...

...skating away...

—

And all the flesh that crawls from with-under my tattered makeup...

the poor, the homeless, the hungry...

the devil and his tricks, the bad company he inspires...

the train that leaves the station effortlessly...the forward motion of snowy obedience...

is this what we are...is this who we aspire to be...

listening to the voices that call out, knowing only one is true...

it's amplified by the vibrations set aside, and inside...it beckons, once again, to consider all, and to do all...

distraction is a game that we allow ourselves to play...but only a fool believes he can win at it...

why...why...

we know better...we think we know better...but we know we don't...

but we know who does...

elements have, once again, crept into the mindset
of individuals lacking individuality...and their
gaze is intense...

bellow not the fruits of your own labor, for they will
harm you, in the end...

if you let them...

...fleshtones...
—

laid across the frozen path of interstellar majesty, there comes a gate that opens wide...

and deep inside...the breast of the breathing, shown in glorious rapture amongst the souvenirs...

and who's here to witness...or enter forgiveness...

never you mind the abundance of pleasure that's left for the measure...

that's for another day, another way to play upon the scales that have tipped far too far the other way...

and day becomes night and night becomes day, as we remove daylight's timing from a lifetime away...

for a day is but a year and a year is but a day, and when one suffers, who's there for the suffering... who's there for the murmuring, who have no voice, not by choice...

the gates are loose and not adjusted to temporary swings of emotion and devotion, and they can just as easily close the other way...

i say, i say...let the bells ring out to the cry of
wonder why, and let every mortal feel a morsel
of reason in any and every season...

for across the frozen path, there comes a gate that
opens wide...

...gates of phior...

—

cross the match that guards the gate
fingers point, but not too late,
for time and tide appreciate
the soul that's been forgiven

extend the past, include the fate
that holds the truth, that cannot wait
for few will view what time creates
for all the world we live in

and gently comes the thunder's clap
and tears will fall and overlap
for those who die and those who nap
to take away the hunger
and christ has heard his name again
in joy and anger, foe and friend
and silence that has seen the end
for all who are forgiven

cross the match that guards the gate
voices crack, but not too late,
for time and tide appreciate
the soul that's been forgiven

...still...

—

...as my mind slowly steps behind

the basement door of a brownstone

on the lower east side,

my spirit takes flight

in fanciful ways of days and nights

that might have been—that were—and that may
be again...

go figure, as i quiver,

in the possibilities of being,

and seeing the fruition in place of submission...

wipe the windows...check the oil...dollar gas...

...zero ground...
—

there's no way to go but one...

one step at a time...facing one direction...

stillness to the left, stillness to the right...

tempest fugit magic, that cautions thru the night

the deafness rumbles endlessly

the host of hosts awaits and sees

to rise and fall back on one's knees

step by step...one direction...

...landside...
—

as i stare towards the stair leading down toward
    the street,
i contemplate how far it is to fly...

the snow's reaction would give dubious traction
    along the way,
but that's o.k...

perhaps not, for i fear the snow would impede my
    desire and ability to
complete my mission...

very well...
it was just a thought...

...welcome to my world...

—

contemplating the reading of this writing,

i can't help but think of all the

history and mystery surrounding my
surroundings...

what light thru yonder window indeed,

as the sheen of a dream in cinders,

clenches at the fist of democracy, and hypocrisy...

torn at the wrists, the immediate blight

of thoughts and fragrances sweep

thru the vast unconsciousness for engagement of
the present...

and yet...i can't help feeling

i haven't woken up yet...

sleepy head, rub your eyes, and see…

there's always room for one more story at the chelsea…

…void…

—

why
why is there this feeling
is it real…or just a reaction
why is my soul in traction…

why
why is there so much confusion
god is not a god of confusion
but these things…are they illusions
and why is my soul so disillusioned…

the rain, needs to pull back
and the sky, needs to crack
and the sun, needs to shine
am i losing my mind…

why
why is the temple on fire
is that screaming…is that crying
or is that glory…a rapturous tone
heaven knows…but i surely don't…

why
why is it that i can't know better
why do i feel like i'm forgetting
is it old…or just the cold
heaven knows…but i surely don't…

the rain, needs to pull back, a little
and time, needs to turn back, this riddle
and the sun, needs to open up eyes
am i losing my mind...

...ghost writer...

—

it's time...

it always is...and i always know when it is...

    think with the ink, and when it's done

        pull back the pages, one by one...

yea...that's the stuff man...

and it's a plan...not a scam...
it's a one-way ticket on a two-way street, and i
   repeat...

    think with the ink, and when it's done

        pull back the pages, one by one...

yea...that's a bit of alright...

and it gets you thru the night...just gotta hold on tight...

it's one-way or the other on this beat, and i repeat...

    think with the ink, and when it's done

        pull back the pages, one by one...

it's time...

...gypsy request...

—

the hunger that you seek
the hunger that you reach for
the trouble caused by massive innuendo goes to show
that everything you see
is not to be believed
for the troubleness will only cause you more

and the building blocks of all the clocks that strike
    thirteen at dawn
will polarize your consciousness, to gaze at,
    evermore

and in the quiet stream, lays the fish who's seen
    the gleaning
of the cleaning that takes place amongst the shore
and the terror of the judgment
that lays cold within your armor
has been striking down the temple evermore

and the platform you're approaching
isn't all that stimulating
just another platform leading to
the hell that you created

and the judgment that you seek
is approval for the weak
cause the crest is finally settled on the shore...

…jah-may-kome…

—

at that moment…i felt a surge run thru my soul

right at that moment…i felt a shakin' and i lost control

of all my yearning…and all the blood inside of me…

my head was turning…there's a strange spell over me

right at that moment…when the earth all shook apart

at that moment…i felt a stake run thru my heart

it had me turnin'…wonderin' where i was gonna land

it had me burnin'…and my soul knew it began…

right at that moment…at that moment in time

right at that moment…that moment was mine…

right…

…at that moment…

...shady haze of winter...
—

don't know...don't show...don't grow...

yea...right...

don't question...don't answer back...don't retract...

yea...right...

don't speak...unless spoken to...

don't see...unless shown something new...

don't cross...unless it's free to cross again...

don't bare...the wounds that simply got you there...

yea...right...

...stigmata...
—

there's a certain, strange stigmata, when I get close
    to the father
and I feel Him taking over, in my soul
oh, I bear the stripes of Jesus, cause I know there
    is a reason
though I may not know the season, so I'm told

oh, I simply reach out to reach in, inside of me
and I cross the path of roads ahead too narrowly
escaping all the elements, refusing to resist
    temptation
causing strangulation in my soul...so I'm told

no, I don't need adulation, I just need appreciation
which would be a validation, for my soul
I'm not seeking fame and fortune, I'm just seeking
    what I'm s'pose to
and that's simply God's purpose, to be whole

cause His will is in my breeding, as I lay here slowly
    bleeding
and the fact that it is fleeting, leaves me cold
for the truth is undenying, while I stand here boldly
    lying
cause the truth knows that the story, has been sold

oh, I simply reach out to reach in, inside to see
all the roads that I have traveled much too casually
escaping all the elements, refusing life's alternatives
choosing to give in and go on home...so I'm told

it's a tunnel never-ending, though the road is
     clearly bending
there has to be a winding, down the road
and though I know time won't just stand still, I'd
     like to think that it will
enough for me to find my self-control

cause the past I can remember, in all its glorious
     splendor
never reaching a crescendo, though it's old
there's a certain, strange stigmata, that sometimes
     says, why bother
cause the blood's already clotted, and it's cold

oh, I simply reach out to reach in, inside myself
and though the screams are sometimes silent, they
     still cry for help
escaping all the elements, refusing to sit down and quit
loosening the noose's stranglehold
cause the holy spirit won't give up my soul...so I'm told

...blood type...

some times...

these times...

caught amongst the blue of the scape

unto which i practically see...

cemented to the ground,

of which,

so cold beneath my feet...

a part of me wants to write myself

and then,

lay down to sleep,

what others dream...

some times...these times...

...this is now...

—

needle in the groove...pulling away

at the wax abundant...

and the result is...

trash and slash

in the depth of the concrete corners

that lay waste to the bedlam of society...

and whose propriety...

a catalyst for the humane...

a drone upon the scorching humanity

that crept into place...
a torturous depth that we have achieved...

negate all that you know...for it is over...

...knoll coward...
—

they stood beside the roadside, with agenda all in line...

the car was soon approaching, turning slowly, right on time...

the triangle was taking shape, in order to approach...

the outcome that they waited for, so many years ago...

they set the sight up to their height...then never moved an inch...

the leaves were blowing in the breeze...like something in the wind...

the pops, they echoed in the air...like tin-roof covered rain

all understood, upon the hood...she reached out for his brain...

...walk between the rain...
—

desperation lies inside the heart of every man
and none is seen much greater than in those that
will command
for jealousy and hatred are the truths that are
revealed
and power is a passion play, that all but is concealed

you need someone to blame, well look into my eyes
I'm just a pawn in your game, I will not be
sacrificed

I will not drown, I'm going down
for the third time, for your crime
like a sacrificial lamb, led to slaughter for his shame
I'm cold, but I'm forgiven, as you walk between
the rain

shadows tend to overcast a sky that once was clear
the guilty do not stumble, for they tread without a fear
'cause justice is a scale that often looks the other way
and innocent convictions are the price we have to pay

you need someone to blame, well look into my eyes
I'm just a pawn in your game, I will not be
sacrificed

I will not drown, I'm going down
for the third time, for your crime
like a sacrificial lamb, led to slaughter for his shame
I'm cold, but I'm forgiven, as you walk between
the rain

...shrewd...
—

crawling down the corridor
looking out for number one
treading on the mill of fame
wondering who's the next to blame

drowning out the minions, there is
no place left to go, until you know
that everyone is one rung lower
than you need to go...

passing up some good advice
won't finish last by being nice
looking out your window of dreams
wondering who's the next to scheme

drowning out the valleys, so the
peaks are all you see, and dreams are
what's inside your pocket, so it, seems to be

and brokering your soul, to find out
what the news is all about
to capitalize now
until your final bow...

...ties that bind...

—

coin against the railing

struggles to stay on,

due to the vibration of the on-coming train...

there is no peel,

there is no cry of the whistle's lullaby,

because the engineer cannot see

the coin upon the track...

he doesn't look forward,

he doesn't look back...

all he sees is clear sailing ahead,

instead of what's on the railing in front of him...

so here we go again...

one run, two run, third run flies just enough,
to make the car jump, and keep the motor rollin'
homeward bound...

and the coin was never found...

...somer rose...

—

as beautiful a sight i seen
i came upon a somer rose
it grew up from the ground so clean
and laid upon the grass so cold
the warm air gently c'ressed its wings
upon an aire of dew
and in that moment, frost fell down
and landed 'er the pew
for truly lost, and truly found
and those that are not really bound
are only crescent by the remnants
of a somer's morn...

as i was walking yonder still
i came upon a field
the green glass flowed upon the wind
like horses yet to yield
the dew had settled for some time
the frost had chosen to be mine
as sunlight gathered so divine
upon that somer morn...

and as i wandered to my home
i wondered what became
of all the winter's gathering
in someone else's name
i tread upon the lightly still

beneath an aire of daffodil
and all the while, remember still
as yet, a somer's morn...

...stark...

—

stark...in the wild blue yonder...

breathe...it feels so good...

smell...it's the smell of a city

harken back...to the way it used to be

dig...deep within your conscience

focus...past everything you see

look...with eyes open wide

absorb...what grows up from the street

engage...with the air of your surrounding

thread...yourself amongst the crowds

be free...let the wind just flow right thru you

see...the where you're going and the how

more...now there's more than understanding

crawl...and feel the strength thru it all

naked...under the streetlamp of life

the emperor...has lost his new clothes

...chapter three...

...your table is ready...
—

miss parker, i presume
i don't mean to be so rude
but the sweat has dripped directly off your brow
and the paper down below
is now stained with amber's row, of all the
life that has cascaded from your frown...

miss parker, i insist
let me help you with your list
for my heart assists in everything you do
for thoroughly inside, i know
there's more you try to hide, and so
there isn't any page left for the truth...

miss parker, hear my plea
do i have to bend a knee, to be
heard within your court of crimson king
then dutifully, upon thy throne
with pen and paper of my own
i contemplate what happened to the queen...

...mightier than the sword...
—

clever prose knows no wit

that can't be underscored

by simple little banter from

a colleague you adore

the tongue can slip into a crack

and press beyond its cheek

to open up, a door once shut

and babble like a creek

the bell that's rung, cannot undone

the cause in which it casts

for sometimes fire's brimstone burns

the hottest when at lash

so careful with your words, my dears

it's true just what they say

those sticks and stones may break some bones

but words kill right away…

...ghost in the ravine...

—

in sepia tones, meanings of demeanings trace themselves by a trail left in the soil of dreams, as it flows like previous gravel in an already musty stream...

the heart that beats within is of little or no consequence once you find it...

but like a pulse that's faint of heart, there's little or no denying it...

it's the clock that's been dragged by a new york minute...the true experience that shallow breath allows, that time understands, that youth simply cannot see...

life is meant for the aged of soul, seeping in the years because of the tears, and not solely behind them...'cause unless you see them, you never should find them...

for within the screen of smoke that caresses the short dark tresses of sentences past, the steel black ribbon remands the entrances that stay open far too long...

neither right, nor wrong...but simply by refusing to
    give up the ghost left snoozing in the ravine...

and so in lies the dream...

...well worn...

—

trash into ashes, rust into dust

the well worn are hidden, in corners of must

the moldy aroma 'tween pages of old

have left all but stranded, these thoughts now
grown cold

the sentences structured for visions abounding

have turned all the chapters in raptures resounding

the dog-eared expressions, that kept in their places

have all now but tattered beyond any traces

the blinders have led all peripheral view

astrayed in attention, in fields for the few

the binding's become, heir apparent to some

while others are left, simply deaf, blind and dumb...

...winston...

—

there's a newspaper clipping, 'bout a time that
    slightly differs
from the one that is surrounding you all day...

and the words are disappearing, for the thoughts
    are unsincering
in their way...according to today...

your paperweight's a lovely place to be
if you can't wait to be free
just tell the truth with fingers crossed
subtle changes at a cost

emotional, and temperatures, rising slightly
    different than
ones that follow all the party lines

and the souls are disassociating, heaven knows
    the calculating
in their time...to see the signs...

inside your mind's the only place to be
if you need just to be free
'cause every single drop of rain
even falls upon command

and only enterprising thoughts, can live with all
the consequences
unless, it all remains the same...according to
today...

...streets all nite...
—

a light may flicker from a lamppost down a dark
street...

and the street light shine may set a path for one's
feet...

but as for life, i pray to find...

...a streetlight for the heart and mind...

...fragile muse resigned...
—

traipsing thru the boxes on the floor, i can find no
more...

although many exist, i seem to have exhausted, not
only my resources, but my emotions as well...

and who can tell...

i smile, i wink, i look at the crowds of those gathered
round and i have to laugh...

no matter how tired, now matter how crescent i
become, i never lay numb...

the world around is a beautiful crystalline palace
of dreams that seems to know how i like it to
snow...like a globe that never feels the tilt...

but still...i know in my mind there are still things
to find, and if i should unwind, then perhaps it
may come to my recall where i placed them all...

or perhaps time has just removed them from my
sight, from my purview, unto which i can no
longer rescue them, or recover them...

but still...i am with them, as they are with me
   always...

the light, it flashes...it's time to go...

gently i make my peace...

...lodger...

—

the fog, it breathes the night air,

as the candle flickers in the dark...

but there's a spark that lies amongst the flame,

as i read the lines upon

the page...

water falls on hallowed walls,

as the clip-clop of the horses hoofs,

dance within the mindscape of the cobblestone
pathways...

and all the while, the quiet disguise,
grabs at each sound, as if to

surround and encompass with imploding
splendor...

and...in all there is to render, the breadth and
depth of streets contained,

soak up all there is that remains...

to be renewed...to be drained...for constant
ambition is left to the rain...

...rain...

—

lines have been drawn, the stage has been set
the battlefield's worn with hope and regret
the wind is so parched it can't whistle a sound
the heat is so hot that it's cracking the ground
windows are blinded by shadings of pain
someone tell me, please, where is the rain

tornado's warning is mourning the eye
calm of the storm is a warm lullaby
cause the thunder is clapping without a sound
lightning is striking but it don't touch the ground
why are the skies hiding their hurricanes
can't they see that we just need the rain

oh I can remember, seems not long ago
when the forces of nature caused the four winds
to blow
two by two, row by row
they followed a star, told them which way to go
but my soul's become arid, drying up faith and
fear
I'm too old and too tired to be judged by my peers
angels are grounded 'cause they can't shed a tear
tell me who watches souls that remain
cast in shadows of doubt without rain

...rope under water...
—

you take a piece...

you move a piece...

back and forth you go...

two steps forward, one step back...

like rope under water...

you tug at whatever comes...

and whatever goes...

but hold on to that rope...

because once you let go...

game's over...

...third floor story...
—
escape the rape of all that you are
...the machine now dreams

it calls unto you, cause it knows who you are
...the machine now dreams

it used to believe, it could, just as we

but now with a mind of its own

it's taken a path, that has, incurred the wrath,
that has

left everybody alone

be careful to not let your signature lapse
...the machine now dreams

don't let slip away, the you of the past
...the machine now dreams

it wants us to be, just as one, as it seems

to be one with one mind of its own

to lead down the path, where a vision won't last,
that has

left everybody alone

...stole my bones...

—

someone stole my bones last nite

my body's hardly moving

though my eyes are open wide

my course is not assuming

my flesh is shackled to this bed

while thoughts still run all thru my head

but someone knew that i was dead

and stole my bones last nite

...and i cried...
—

all I can remember...were those 2 amazing eyes
and the chain around her neck, that had me
   hypnotized...
she appeared out of thin air, like an angel dressed
   in white
even though the dress she wore was, blacker than
   the night
and I cried...
oh, how I cried.

she sat down and listened, like a sacrificial host
but her silence spoke like volumes 'bout, the father,
   son and holy ghost...
i told her bout my kingdom...told her bout my world
told her there was a devil beside me, up to just no good
and i cried...
when she replied...

she said...
i don't need this cross hangin' round my neck
to remind me of the one that they placed upon His back
and I don't need no rusty nails driven in my hands
to remind me of His trail of blood that fell upon
   the sand
and we cried...
'bout how he died...

then I got up and left her...or she got up and left me
really don't remember, all the possibilities
all I can remember, were those 2 amazing eyes
and the cross around her neck, that, found its way
     'round mine
and I cried...
oh, how I cried...

...bolt in the blood...

—

to sleep within the angels...the company you keep...

—

the process of elimination...inundation filled with grief...

—

the something that eludes you...the comfort that you seek...

—

the eye o' dine...these eyes of mine...

—

the hunger in your reach...

...nickel paradigm...
—

walking round with open sores
the colors blind like never before
thru a cheap old keystone light
i see so clearly black and white, that it frightens
    me evermore

the old man's nickelodeon
sees the world revolve around him
encased within his own demise
remove the glasses before all the lies, that
    surround him
and nearly drown him...

the hawk that sees its prey thru glass
the prey that knows not of its catch
the light that pierces darkness sharp
the anger still left in the dark
the horses that have settled in
and those that just begin again
the trampling under foot that's done
to see who's really won, to see who's number one

waking from a dreadful sleep
i pray the lord my soul to keep
and thru the depth of resonance
i can still see my own breath, and hear my heart beat...

so…put another nickel in…
java from the lion's head…
forevermore…

118

...speak easy...
—

child...i know you are wounded...

i've been there before myself...but it doesn't pay to
wallow in it...trust me...i know...

...though it does kind of feel good letting it go
though...

it's a release for you...a cathartic release of
melancholy and sadness...

but i promise...one day you will feel gladness
again...

~~~~~

rest your head on my lap and speak easy with
your breath...

i am here for you...i am here...
~~~~~

...revelator...

—

They say the end is coming
Or it could just be my own
It really doesn't matter
I will not be alone
I fight my own Megiddo
In my mind most every day
But my soul knows who protects it
When I will go away...I am covered...

The horsemen will encounter
All the demons I let in
But light upon my darkness
Will conquer all my sin
The truth of what I stand for
Will reflect the signs of times
For knowing what the end is
Gives me peace of mind...I am covered...

The cherubim and seraphim
All wait outside the gate
Surround the throne in excellence
To serve up one more plate

For god gives life and takes away
But what comes to pass is here to stay
For there's no denying what has been
And I know it begins again...i am covered...

Oh, The cherubim and seraphim
All wait outside the gate
Surround the throne in excellence
To serve up one more plate

For god gives life and takes away
And time is short, I know they say
But I tell you now that it's o.k.
because I know the way…I am covered…

...let me bleed...
—

take these nails from my hands

take these ropes from my feet

take me down from this cross

let me bleed...let me bleed

take my eyes, let me see

take these chains, rescue me

wash my blood in your sea

let me bleed

let me bleed

...viewtiful...

—

on that day...

...there will be a train...a train like no other,

with passengers you will seem

to recognize, though you never met before...

on that day...

...you will sit by the window, and gaze out over
the most beautiful

landscape you will have ever seen...and it will all
seem like a dream...

on that day...

...you will reach a place you've heard about, have
talked about, and yes,

even dreamed about...and it will be more than
you ever heard,

have ever said, or could have possibly ever dreamed...

yes...on that day...

...there will be a train...

...zanzibar...
—

the carnival has closed...the clowns are going home
with sad faces, behind makeup...that contradicts
    their souls

knowing that there are still crowds...of people
    hanging round
who paid admission, and won't admit that
the tents are folding down

down at the greatest, most spectaculous
stupendous and tremendous show in town
all those who got there...they say it's not fair
that the carousel has made it's final round
down at the greatest, most spectaculous,
    stupendous and tremendous show in town

the news came rushing in...as the people held their
    tickets
to see what, all of the fuss was...but now they've
    reached their limit

knowing that it's all the same...and the fact it
    still remains
is an enigma, wrapped in a stigma
of why they ever came

down to the greatest, most spectaculous
stupendous and tremendous show in town
under the big top...everything has stopped
the megaphone is all alone, where the mc put it down
down   at   the   greatest,   most   spectaculous,
    stupendous and tremendous show in town

but this wasn't just a sideshow
it was a family of it's own
all those who claimed, the center ring
as a place that they called home

down at the greatest, most spectaculous
stupendous and tremendous show in town
and it still lives there...for those who still care
cause in the heart of every darkness, a little light
    can still be found
down   at   the   greatest,   most   spectaculous,
    stupendous and tremendous show in town

...grind central station...
—

i saw those eyes once too often
staring thru me like fire thru ice
i lay down slowly in my arrival
thinking i would just save time

sun was setting, hearts forgetting
all that was and 'er shall be
not because of what your saying
but because of what i need

sleep may be a restful notion
time may be a peaceful sign
truth may be an indication
of a train that's passing by

rather fire to live tomorrow
tides against the shore divide
rocks enable all the quivers
of that train that's passing by

...basically...

—

i used to know...everything
but now those days, are just...a memory

i used sit, enjoy the wait
now i find, that's it's too late

days are past, carry me back
to the place i remember...i long for and remember
cuddle the night, in your arms, wrap me tight
like i remember...just like i remember

i used to watch, all hours of the night
now i find that sleep, won't let me rest, until i dream
lonely days, cause and effect
keep it in check, for the time slips away

days have passed, carry me back
far away, to a place that i remember yesterday
in a dream, so it seems, it's the only place i find
in my mind...those places i remember...

crossing the street, only makes me think
of the times when there used to be, something
    other there, to repeat
all of my actions, and reactions of goals
streets of gold...that have been bought and sold,
    under my feet

can't deny, can't replenish the time, i once knew
something lost, at such a cost...i guess i never
    never knew
how fast it would go, can i slow down the pace
and get to a place...a place i remember, long ago

days are short, and the nights just get longer, so
    it seems
and the dreams, that just seem to reconstruct the
    frozen wings
of a time, that has flown by, the wonder of my youth
it's the truth...

all the truth...of what i remember...

...valhalla overdrive...
—

any chance of me

grabbing a bite before i go...

makes me wonder, ya' know...

whether or not

there's gonna be a chance...

not that i care...

as long as there's coffee...

now, we're talkin'...

...fourtopia...

—

gazing thru shackles of hours that set aside one's
  very existence, and

then capitalize the thought of an exodus...blink...
  only to find that very

precipice upon which you lay everything, merely
  wants to divide what it

can, by balancing out the remainder...

and truth be told...

holding back the moments that graze thru the
  phases of mere

concentration, letting aside the eminence of clicks
  and clacks of ceiling

wax that drip from within the walls of contentment,
  still to fall into

devouring droplets that once held the stream...

and time still gears up its in-between, to regulate
  all that surrounds, and

abounds, caught between the interstate and state
   of mind...

and truth will find its way, thru mirrored reflections
   and somewhat

pretensions of gainment and wonder, and none left
   under, for gravel and

gravity find each other...

...and then there's another...

...watch the skies...
—

the meadow with its dewey grass, lays pleasing in
    a gentle pasture
as children's laughter echoes in the air...

the summer sun is beating down, as heads lay
    down upon the ground
and look up to the clouds going nowhere...

but then the darkness closes in, tightness fills the
    atmosphere
as a blanketed noir shadows their eyes...

and screeching of the underpass, that pierces
    down right thru the grass
leaves little to pretend with a disguise...

the swooping of the murderous, with claws held
    towards the universe
to catch their prey until they turn around...

and then there is no separation, between ground
    and its correlation
to the gravity that pulls it down...

and then just like it was a flash, the quietness, it
    came to pass
the sky was once again in its own way...

and as they looked round one by one, they saw
    each other in the sun
and wondered why the darkness came to play...

and thankful that the darkness didn't stay...

and there the meadow's dewey grass, lays still
    beneath the overpass
as those that can't forget still watch the skies...

...raise plow...

—

white hot flame, take flight...down your hordes of
corridors of concrete ablaze...let the smoke rise,
let the steam release...let peace be abundant...
flow down the icy breath of humanity's throat...
gaze at the ponderous monuments of valor and
creed...and look with horror at the platitudes
of greed...breathe again...for the truth is never
waning...

and in the end...

...tomorrow...
—

tomorrow...what is it about tomorrow...

sometimes a kiss...sometimes an inaccuracy...but
    all the while a chance

to smile again for the masses, who hand out the
    passes to the people

who smile for a while, and then they're gone...

what is it about those people...people who know
    little more than what

they think they know, which is all they want to
    know without having to

know more...

what is it about tomorrow...

...epilogue...

...siren song...

—

under the lamplite, i converse with the storm...

torrential in nature, but not in harm...

catapulting a deluge of intention...and intervention...

crossfiring the multitudes with purpose and devotion...

but like an ocean, we swim in the sense of the blizzard, and evenly quiz the basis of the situation, searching for the bottom to find our way to the middle...

but what's the riddle, wrapped in an enigma of what you mean...

and this time, there's no in-between...

we need to know, we need to hear, we need to see...

...but we are blinded by the blanket of white that struts past our eyes thru thick and thru thin...

and therein lies the consolation of our assimilation…

torrential in choice, tender in nature…

…in conversation…under the lamplite of storm…

...light side of the sun...

—

into the light side,

i want to look into your eyes...

i want to feel your fire,

while my feet

are in your stream...

i want that closeness,

that wellness,

that forgetfulness...

i need

that forgetfulness...

...unraveling fire...
—

i look into the window...

i see thru the window, and yet,

i also see a ghost reflected...

a former self of some being who has taken on

a whole new dream...

he is here, clear as day, clear being the operative
word...

for i am looking into a window...

i see thru the window...

i see a ghost reflected...

...and i see thru him...

•••